MUSEUM of

LOST and

BROKEN THINGS

LAUREN TERRY

Leafe Press

Leafe Press
4 Cohen Close
Chilwell
Nottingham
NG9 6RW
England

Copyright © Lauren Terry, 2020. All rights reserved.

Cover photograph: "Louisiana after Hurricane Katrina: Scene in flood devastated St. Bernard Parish residential area." Owner / photographer: Infrogmation https://commons.wikimedia.org/wiki/User:Infrogmation)
© Copyright Infrogmation and licensed for reuse under Creative Commons Licence.

ISBN: 978-1-9999451-4-5

CONTENTS

The Sleeping Woman is a Cubist Portrait	5
Bagless Cylinder Vacuum	6
Catalogue Item: 24	7
Play-Doh Man	8
The Eyeless Birds	9
Catalogue Item: 137	10
Cruise Ship	11
Cubist Portrait of a Three-Faced Doll	12
Dream House	13
Beehive (Thimble Forest)	15
Catalogue Item: 7	16
Soft Boiled Egg	17
The Other Side of an Apple	18
Catalogue Item: 283	19
High-Rise	20
How to Smooth Pink Anaglypta	21
Catalogue Item: 579	22
Evergreen Crematorium	23
Worry Dolls	24
Red Balloon	25
Catalogue Item: 33	26
Beachcombing in the Torres Strait	27
Tramping the Sods with Uncle Mellie	28
Bébé Marie	29
Catalogue Item: 1	30

For Adam

The Sleeping Woman is a Cubist Portrait

Semblance of an unexpended artillery shell,
or unlit table lamp, shade nodding.

She has come apart, a soiled dinner plate –
shattered, stinking, spilling geometric shapes
from the bed's single frame.

Her members are pure assemblage:
rivet, tongue, and cane.

A plastic butter knife
detaches
reattaches itself
at an obscene angle –

one pinion limp beneath the sheets,
the other hailing the thing beyond the ceiling.

Bagless Cylinder Vacuum

feed it pins for the gullet is crush-proof lurching its vociferations cordless tempest space of devoid matter flat square head tonguing cat hair and the gullet is choke-proof feed it coins confetti disks and hold lock button to lift dust cup to easy empty gut of human skin or hosiery space devoid of matter churning mites and spiders scale the gullet when you sup or strip legs from the body is a black ball to plug the gut is fool-proof feed it pins to pick its teeth leg of a clothes peg pen cap bottle cap battery pack balloon clip and six loose teeth from a comb pull along your space of devoid matter lurching three-year warranty bottom feeder can you stomach it

Catalogue Item: 24

bear with glass eyes
cataracts are a sure sign of age

Play-Doh Man

He cuts a big red tongue,
sticks it to his chin and sets it flapping –

soft blue pats flattened
on his nail plates,

a fat orange eye (yellow yolk)
in his bony cup.

When he hoots, slick green peas
fall out and the plaque tastes like salt.

The Eyeless Birds

Lithe-winged bodies snagged
on the silver head of a pin;

they flee from death at obscene angles –

do not remember
the motion of flight,

belly-up, hindlimbs cinched in sisal twine.

Scissor-beaked
and dried like pitted fruit –

the eye is a black pip, hole plugged with cotton wool,

because children should not think
of death in cabinets,

pointing at the nothing on the other side of the glass.

Catalogue Item: 137

chain of paperclips
red orange pink and blue
the pattern loops

Cruise Ship

At the lip of the sea,
a fat white body
is snagged on capstone,
flank slick with algae.

A boy prods
its belly with a stick,
and swears
he sees it flinch.

Cubist Portrait of a Three-Faced Doll

when it shrieks the head spins right round to match a face to keening baby is a simple oscillation of sleep and mirth and oh the weeping pity the pretty little thing which cannot match name to thing to three mouths six eyes and four good for seeing baby which does not know its face from a thing in a mirror and baby's head spins right round to match a face to gurgling baby is a monstrous little thing with joins around the edges where baby comes apart the skull is a soft white thing and baby does not like it when you shake its head gets caught between sleep and mirth and babbling imperfect symmetry its bulging head six eyes a button nose for every pair the thing a mother should not love and when it bawls the head spins right round to match a face to name an oscillation is a pretty monstrous thing

Dream House
after Gaston Bachelard

where tacky carpets pluck
the shoes from your feet

she slams the door so
hard the knob falls off

where black mould eats
orange matte emulsion

wipe it down with foggy water
grey dishcloth in a pail

watch shadows move
between the rooms

where sheets
make ghosts of cabinets

slice the line of tape
to let things breathe

and do not use her flannel
for fear of smelling lavender

where clingfilm wraps
the body of the tub

an uncapped drain
dribbles yellow

and squirrels gnaw wires
in the crawlspace

she keeps the house awake
at night chattering

cardboard chipboard
cupboard clipboard

paint your name beside others
beneath the wallpaper

watch hot breath
leave her body

and know that in this cavity
there was once a wall

Beehive (Thimble Forest)
after Joseph Cornell

Shrink your eye
to match the aperture of a pinhole
and tally pitted tankers
snagged on pylons –
lurching over badlands,
where planets rove in circles
in the cambered pit of a mirrored drum.

Hold your tongue
and the pylons reverberate –
the silver whine of a carillon bell
slicing *ad infinitum*
through the blankness.

Catalogue Item: 7

chatter telephone
rolls its eyes
no body
on the line's
other end

Soft Boiled Egg

With the silver comes
a splitting –
white yawning flaps
begin to spit
their yellow pus.

Nestled at the core,
a grey and steaming thing

is sheathed
in porous film –
unblinking
achromatic
eyes.

The Other Side of an Apple

imagine the other face is flat or blue in a bowl of other fruits with various other names split the apple clean in half and in the ovary there are pits for such pits on the hot wet mound of your tongue things resemble apples pregnant apples in form or colour on the other face is there a knife in its back is there a tooth or bot fly feasting shrunken head or abstract flatness god do not touch it imagine god is an apple do not bash it spit god into the palm of your right hand and let it drop lunar ball the fall might kill it spill its pips the push would make it flat on its other face

Catalogue Item: 283

silver bell cannot know
where it left its tongue

High-Rise
after Joseph Cornell's Compartmented Box

what keeps the boy
at his window
is the ball on its sill
rocking

as if the ball believed
it could not fall
and the body believed
it could not follow

How to Smooth Pink Anaglypta

Scratch papule-heads
from epidermis;

between thumb and forefinger
make a paste;

spread on curtain,
cup, or chair;

then, dig the reek of damp
from your nailbeds;

*(if you licked it,
it would taste like salt)*

plug the pores
with Calamine, No. 230;

*(let it form a crust,
like cradle cap)*

file it down,
inhale the dust;

repeat
for the wall.

Catalogue Item: 579

pencil nibs
in a sandwich bag
would not be made
to sharpen

Evergreen Crematorium

white cottage on a wooded hill flue burning white seeping from an open window when the door is locked white cottage leaks the breath it had been holding lidded boxes wait in lines their fearful symmetry flue smoking flesh in boxes bone to white grit and other boxes wait in line for bodies bother other bodies when cardboard is cheaper than wood and cottage cheaper than grave when flowers give their bodies to names the body cannot know their sagging forms diggers breaking ground they dare not think of bodies and the thing on the wooded hill is just a cottage white light flue burning

Worry Dolls

We are six
little bodies
in a pouch –

peg-legged,

we wear straitjackets,

black dots
for eyes.

Behemoth,
you come by moonlight –
wet tongue

flapping
testaments

we will not tell,

because our lips
are sutured
shut.

Loosen the cord
and let us slip,

headfirst

into your sticky palm.

Red Balloon

or shrunken head (partially severed
cord) or amorphous glove (no holes to insert
digits) or cut of uterine endometrium (raw
cochineal gristle) or contraceptive diaphragm
(silicone dome) or blood moon (remote prophetic
disk) or congealed soup (gelatinous skin) or

Catalogue Item: 33

heap of wax fruits in a bowl
unsuited to human consumption

Beachcombing in the Torres Strait

Washed-up fishing net
slumps on hot sand –

a half-buried bottle
lies uncapped,
bottom-up
in the dune grass.

The flesh-footed shearwater
is on its back, rocking –
belly sliced at the core.

These are the sticky fragments
of sharp, discarded things:

ring pull; leg of a clothes peg; seaglass; pen cap; bottle cap; pipe cap;
balloon clip; six loose teeth from a comb.

It's trachea
Is a bendy straw
half-crushed
underfoot.

Tramping the Sods with Uncle Mellie

Three metal shacks
piled on a yellow mound,
silent and hulking.

You stand on tip-toes, poke
your fingers through the slats –

push your nose
against wet sheets
and gape.

Uncle Mellie jabs one with his stick,
makes the whole thing judder.

He will not let you close
enough to pet
their bald red heads,

or ask them how
they lost their tongues.

Bébé Marie
after Joseph Cornell

When Marie's dress turns
the sour yellow of bad milk,

I take her out to the thicket
at the foot of our apple tree.

Because Marie's head goes around and around,
she wears her collar high to hide the deep black slit

where her swan's neck
and pretty head should meet.

When night falls, Marie taps at my window –
begging to come home.

But the grinding of her joints keeps me up,
and I pull Marie's arms from their sockets

to put them in a box,
should she ever need them again.

Marie's eyes are black craters in a full moon,
and she is gone by morning.

Because she is not sorry,
I lop Marie's hair with scissors

and when she weeps, I kiss her little nose –
poke flowers through her straw hat.

I bury Marie, face-down, in the thicket
at the foot of our apple tree.

Catalogue Item: 1

unfinished birdbox
no roof
no windows
no door

www.ingramcontent.com/pod-product-compliance
Lightning Source LLC
LaVergne TN
LVHW051923060526
838201LV00060B/4154